BRITISH RAILWAYS STEAMING ON THE LONDON MIDLAND REGION

Volume Five

Compiled by
PETER HANDS

DEFIANT PUBLICATIONS
190 Yoxall Road
Shirley, Solihull
West Midlands

Printed on behalf of Richard Netherwood Limited, by Gorenjski tisk p.o. Slovenia.

CURRENT STEAM PHOTOGRAPH ALBUMS AVAILABLE FROM DEFIANT PUBLICATIONS

VOLUME 14
A4 size - Hardback. 96 pages
-178 b/w photographs.
£14.95 + £1.50 postage.
ISBN 0 946857 40 7.

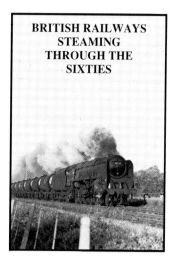

VOLUME 15
A4 size - Hardback. 96 pages
-178 b/w photographs.
£16.95 + £1.50 postage.
ISBN 0 946857 52 0.

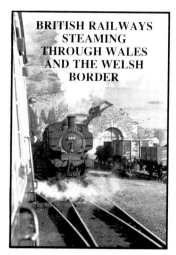

A4 size - Hardback. 96 pages
-175 b/w photographs.
£17.95 + £1.50 postage.
ISBN 0 946857 56 3.

VOLUME 1
A4 size - Hardback. 96 pages
-177 b/w photographs.
£14.95 + £1.50 postage.
ISBN 0 946857 41 5.

BRITISH RAILWAYS
STEAMING
IN THE
NORTH WEST

IN
PREPARATION

BRITISH RAILWAYS
STEAMING
IN THE
SOUTH WEST

IN
PREPARATION

VOLUME 11
A4 size - Hardback. 96 pages
-176 b/w photographs.
£16.95 + £1.50 postage.
ISBN 0 946857 48 2.

VOLUME 12
A4 size - Hardback. 96 pages
-176 b/w photographs.
£16.95 + £1.50 postage.
ISBN 0 946857 49 0.

VOLUME 1
A4 size - Hardback. 96 pages
-177 b/w photographs.
£14.95 + £1.50 postage.
ISBN 0 946857 39 3.

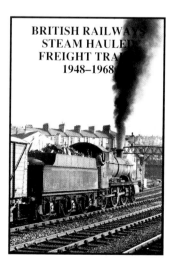

VOLUME 1
A4 size - Hardback. 96 pages
-174 b/w photographs.
£14.95 + £1.50 postage.
ISBN 0 946857 42 3.

VOLUME 1
A4 size - Hardback. 96 pages
-179 b/w photographs.
£15.95 + £1.50 postage.
ISBN 0 946857 43 I.

BRITISH RAILWAYS
STEAMING
THROUGH THE
SIXTIES

IN
PREPARATION

VOLUME 16

FUTURE STEAM PHOTOGRAPH ALBUMS
AND OTHER TITLES

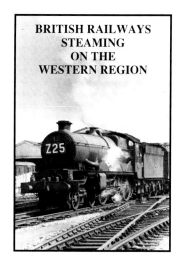

BRITISH RAILWAYS
STEAMING
ON THE
WESTERN REGION

VOLUME 4
A4 size - Hardback. 96 pages
-177 b/w photographs.
£15.95 + £1.50 postage.
ISBN 0 946857 46 6.

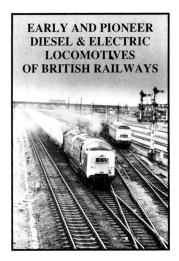

EARLY AND PIONEER
DIESEL & ELECTRIC
LOCOMOTIVES
OF BRITISH RAILWAYS

A4 size - Hardback. 96 pages
-177 b/w photographs.
£15.95 + £1.50 postage.
ISBN 0 946857 45 8.

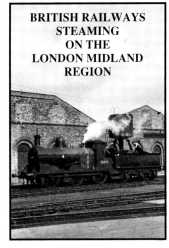

BRITISH RAILWAYS
STEAMING
ON THE
LONDON MIDLAND
REGION

VOLUME 4
A4 size - Hardback. 96 pages
-177 b/w photographs.
£15.95 + £1.50 postage.
ISBN 0 946857 47 4.

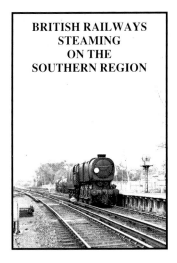

BRITISH RAILWAYS
STEAMING
ON THE
SOUTHERN REGION

VOLUME 3
A4 size - Hardback. 96 pages
-177 b/w photographs.
£17.95 + £1.50 postage.
ISBN 0 946857 54 7.

BRITISH RAILWAYS
STEAM HAULED
TITLED TRAINS

A4 size - Hardback. 96 pages
-169 b/w photographs.
£16.95 + £1.50 postage.
ISBN 0 946857 51 2.

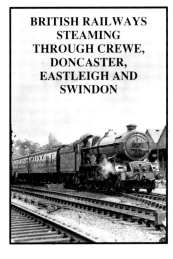

BRITISH RAILWAYS
STEAMING
THROUGH CREWE,
DONCASTER,
EASTLEIGH AND
SWINDON

A4 size - Hardback. 96 pages
-179 b/w photographs.
£17.95 + £1.50 postage.
ISBN 0 946857 53 9.

BRITISH RAILWAYS
STEAMING
THROUGH LONDON

A4 size - Hardback. 96 pages
-174 b/w photographs.
£17.95 + £1.50 postage.
ISBN 0 946857 55 5.

BRITISH RAILWAYS
STEAMING ON
THE EX-LNER
LINES

VOLUME 4
A4 size - Hardback. 96 pages
-183 b/w photographs.
£17.95 + £1.50 postage.
ISBN 0 946857 57 1.

BRITISH RAILWAYS
STEAMING FROM
1948–1968

'50th' ALBUM
A4 size - Hardback. 96 pages
-186 b/w photographs.
£16.95 + £1.50 postage.
ISBN 0 946857 50 4.

BRITISH RAILWAYS
STEAMING
ON THE
LONDON MIDLAND
REGION

VOLUME 5
A4 size - Hardback. 96 pages.
- 177 b/w photographs.
£17.95 + £1.50 postage.
ISBN 0 946857 58X.

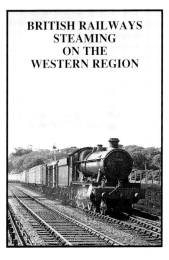

BRITISH RAILWAYS
STEAMING
ON THE
WESTERN REGION

VOLUME 5
A4 size - Hardback. 96 pages.
- 177 b/w photographs.
£17.95 + £1.50 postage.
ISBN 0 946857 59 8.

It's a dog's life in the
FIRE SERVICE
by Peter St.Bernard

COMEDY
269 pages. Cartoons.
£9.95 + £1.00 postage.
ISBN 0 946857 30 X.

ACKNOWLEDGEMENTS

Grateful thanks are extended to the following contributors of photographs not only for their use in this book but for their kind patience and long term loan of negatives/photographs whilst this book was being compiled.

T.R.AMOS TAMWORTH	K.BARROW * *	W.BOYEN BEXHILL
R.BUTTERFIELD MIRFIELD	R.S.CARPENTER BIRMINGHAM	S.DARTNELL DERBY
KEN ELLIS SWINDON	A.N.H.GLOVER BIRMINGHAM	B.K.B.GREEN WARRINGTON
RAY HARRIS NEW MALDEN	PETER HAY HOVE	MIKE HIGSON THE SMOKEBOX
R.W.HINTON GLOUCESTER	I.J.HODSON CAMBRIDGE	F.HORNBY NORTH CHEAM
A.C.INGRAM WISBECH	D.K.JONES MOUNTAIN ASH	T.LEWIS *
R.PICTON WOLVERHAMPTON	N.E.PREEDY GLOUCESTER	A.RANKIN BARRHEAD
J.SCHATZ LITTLETHORPE	C.P.STACEY STONY STRATFORD	M.S.STOKES MARPLE
J.M.TOLSON BIGGLESWADE	TERRY WARD NORTHAMPTON	D.WEBSTER *
KIT WINDLE LOWER BREDBURY		

 * Courtesy of the Norman Preedy collection.
 ** Courtesy of Colin Stacey

Front Cover - Under clear signals LMS Class 5 4-6-0 No. 44737, from 24E Blackpool, hurries past a weed-strewn embankment as it passes through Leyland station to the south of Preston with a local passenger working on an August day in 1957. Leyland station, once jointly owned by the London & North Western Railway and the Lancashire & Yorkshire Railway (North Union Joint) is 205 miles from London (Euston) and was once famous for its car manufacturing industry. (N.E.Preedy)

ISBN 0 946857 58 X

(C) P.B.HANDS 1997
FIRST PUBLISHED 1997

INTRODUCTION

BRITISH RAILWAYS STEAMING ON THE LONDON MIDLAND REGION - Volume 5 is the fifth book to concentrate on the London Midland Region of British Railways. Included in this book are photographs take at locations in Scotland which were once part of the LMS. This fifth album contains a wide and varied selection of photographs provided by some twenty-nine contributors of steam at work and rest from over one hundred different locations on the London Midland Region and Scotland from 1948 until 1968 when allocated steam on the region ceased. Some areas of greater interest, such as Carlisle, Crewe, Derby and Manchester have been given more coverage than others.

These books are designed to give the ordinary, everyday steam photographic enthusiast of the 1950's and 1960's a chance to participate in and give pleasure to others whilst recapturing the twilight days of steam.

Apart from the main 1950's and 1960's series, further individual albums like this one will be produced from time to time. Wherever possible, no famous names will be found nor will photographs which have been published before be used. Nevertheless, the content and quality of the majority of photographs selected will be second to none.

The majority of photographs used in this album have been contributed by readers of Peter Hands series of booklets entitled "What Happened to Steam" and "BR Steam Shed Allocations" (both still available) and from readers of the earlier "BR Steaming Through The Sixties" albums. Under normal circumstances these may have been hidden from the public eye for ever.

The continuation of the "BR Steaming" series etc., depends upon you the reader. If you wish to join my mailing list for future albums and/or feel you have suitable material of BR steam locomotives between 1948-1968 and wish to contribute them towards this series and other albums, please contact:-

Tel No.
0121 745-8421

Peter Hands,
190 Yoxall Road,
Shirley, Solihull,
West Midlands B90 3RN

CONTENTS

Memories of the London Midland Region and Scotland

1) Upper quadrant signals at Lichfield (Trent Valley) in 1957. (R.S.Carpenter)

2) Interior of Bletchley booking office on 27th December 1954. (K.Barrow)

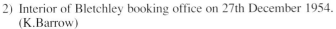

3) 8H Birkenhead ash and coal plants on 29th May 1966. (C.P.Stacey)

4) 12A Carlisle (Kingmoor) from the north on 30th August 1964. (D.K.Jones)

5) A 1950's shed view of Forfar. (R.Butterfield)

6) Framed by a well placed tree, LMS Class 5 4-6-0 No 45105, from 12A Carlisle (Kingmoor), is seen passing over Dillicar water troughs in the Lune Valley with a northbound goods train on a sunny 12th May 1966. A once longstanding resident of 26A Newton Heath, No 45105 served from 27C Southport from January 1961 until January 1963. It then moved to 12C Carlisle (Canal) for six months before arriving at Kingmoor. It survived until October 1966. (N.E.Preedy)

7) The glass panes in the massive station roof at Manchester (London Road) have been blackened by the smoke of countless steam engines over the years as 9B Stockport allocated LMS Fowler Class 4 2-6-4T No 42353, bearing the logo of its former owner, departs with a local passenger train on 10th April 1953. To the right of No 42353 is LNER B1 Class 4-6-0 No 61124 which is a visitor to Manchester from the Eastern Region, being shedded at 36A Doncaster. (B.K.B.Green)

8) Fully coaled and in steam, LMS Class 4P Compound 4-4-0 No 40933 awaits its next duty as it stands alongside the former London & North Western six-road shed at 3E Monument Lane in Birmingham on 7th September 1953. Situated on the west side of the tunnel from Birmingham (New Street) on the Wolverhampton (High Level) line, Monument Lane closed completely on 12th February 1962 with the locos and men moving to Aston shed. (B.K.B.Green)

9) Ex. Caledonian Railway Pickersgill Class 3P 4-4-0 No 54485 (63A Perth) stands beneath the lattice-work pedestrian footbridge at Crieff station on 18th June 1960 with a joint SLS/RCTS special from Perth, complete with a restored Caledonian Railway coach next to the engine. The Comrie to Gleneagles via Crieff branch closed in 1964 as did the associated stations at Pittenzie Halt, Highlandman, Strageath Halt, Muthill and Tullibardine. (F.Hornby)

10) With the large goods shed and yard in the background, former Midland Railway Class 3F 0-6-0 No 43565 wheezes and clanks its way onto the main line at Bedford which is guarded by a pair of upper quadrant signals on a damp-looking 7th November 1961. No 43565, based locally at 14E, is in charge of a pick-up freight. Transferred to Bedford shed from 14C St.Albans in January 1959, No 43565 was withdrawn in June 1962 and cut up at Derby Works. (T.R.Amos)

11) A few short months after nationalisation and LMS *Jubilee* Class 4-6-0 No 5698 *Mars* is beautifully lined out with the letters LMS freshly painted on its tender. *Mars*, later renumbered 45698, is standing in front of the large running shed at 25F Low Moor on 2nd May 1948. At the end of 1956 Low Moor became the property of the North Eastern Region, being coded 56F until closure in October 1967, two years after *Mars* was withdrawn. (A.N.H.Glover)

12) Following heavy overhauls, LMS engines gleam and glisten in their new coats of paint deep within the mighty workshops at Crewe on 10th June 1951. Nearest the camera is Class 4 2-6-4T No 42547, from 24B Rose Grove, which survived in service until May 1963. In the right background is *Princess* Class 4-6-2 No 46210 *Lady Patricia* which will soon be returned home to 5A Crewe (North). Towards the end of its life *Lady Patricia* was drafted to 66A Polmadie (Glasgow) where it worked from July 1958 to March 1961. (B.K.B.Green)

9

13) A panoramic view of part of Stafford station with its grimy canopy on 29th November 1953 where we espy a 'stranger-in-the-camp'. Under clear signals GWR *Castle* Class 4-6-0 No 5015 *Kingswear Castle*, of 84A Wolverhampton (Stafford Road), snakes its way past Stafford No 6 signalbox with an express bound for Paddington during diversions owing to the rebuilding of Shifnal Bridge. In the left of the frame we can make out part of Stafford shed. (R.S.Carpenter)

14) This spotless LMS Class 4P Compound No 40914, pictured in the shed yard at 67A Corkerhill (Glasgow) in between two other engines on 5th August 1951, is one of some twenty examples of the class stationed in the former Glasgow & South Western Railway area at this date in time. No 40914 was a product of the locomotive builders at the Vulcan Foundry in 1927 and gave twenty-seven years of service before withdrawal in September 1954. (B.K.B.Green)

15) A busy scene in the yard at 12B Carlisle (Upperby) shed on 6th September 1964. In the foreground is the front end of an LMS Class 5 4-6-0, two LMS Class 3F 0-6-0 Tanks, one being No 47345 and an unidentified LMS Class 2 2-6-0. Despite being in steam No 47345 was withdrawn from Upperby later in the month. To the left of No 47345 is the long condemned (November 1962) LMS *Princess* Class 4-6-2 No 46200 *The Princess Royal* in fading maroon livery. (A.Rankin)

16) A host of semaphore signals guard the busy tracks at New Mills South Junction as LMS Class 4F 0-6-0 No 44185 disturbs the peaceful countryside as it blasts along with a seemingly endless rake of empty mineral wagons on a summer's day on 16th June 1951. From a class first introduced into service in 1924, No 44185 was a long-term inhabitant of 21A Saltley, eventually moving on to 9G Gorton in May 1964, six months prior to withdrawal and oblivion. (B.K.B.Green)

17) A crowded setting at Heaton Norris Junction with a fine assortment of signals, yards, a signalbox and two trains. LMS Class 3 2-6-2T No 40081 (9B Stockport) on a Stockport to Manchester (London Road) local passenger overtakes LMS Class 8F 2-8-0 No 48289, from 5B Crewe (South), which is hauling an express freight on 27th July 1953. No 40081 took its leave of 9B in March 1958, moving to 11A Carnforth. It survived until October 1961. (B.K.B.Green)

18) Looking extremely smart in its shining black paint and red buffers, former Caledonian Railway Class 2F 0-6-0 No 57287 stands devoid of coal stocks between two LMS engines alongside the wooden coaling stage at Glasgow's St.Rollox shed (65B) on 6th April 1958. Based at 65F Grangemouth, No 57287 has just emerged from St.Rollox Works after what must have been its last general repair. Withdrawn in November 1961 it was cut up twelve months later. (Peter Hay)

19) Steam locomotives abound in this picture taken at 17A Derby on a sunny 19th August 1951. Amongst the ones on show is an LMS Class 8F 2-8-0, and two LMS Class 5 4-6-0's (one being of the Caprotti variety). Posing on the open turntable is LMS Class 2P 4-4-0 No 40632, an engine native to 17A, which has BRITISH RAILWAYS stencilled on its tender. No 40632 ended its days allocated to 16A Nottingham, being condemned in February 1961. (B.K.B.Green)

20) Begrimed LMS *Royal Scot* Class 4-6-0 No 46144 *Honourable Artillery Company*, a 5A Crewe (North) steed, is in the twilight of its illustrious career as it is relegated to the more mundane duty of hauling a down fitted freight, seen here passing a pile of sleepers at Bletchley in September 1963. *Honourable Artillery Company*, once a longstanding resident of 1B Camden, was withdrawn from 5A in January 1964 and scrapped at Crewe Works the same month. (I.J.Hodson)

21) Two grimy members of the once numerous ranks of the LMS Class 8F 2-8-0's stand tender to tender in the all but deserted shed yard at 10F Rose Grove on 14th June 1968, one of the last surviving bastions of steam on British Railways. Nearest the camera is No 48191 newly transferred to Rose Grove from 9F Heaton Mersey with 10F crudely stencilled on its smokebox door. Condemned in August 1968, No 48191 was cut up at the end of the year. (N.E.Preedy)

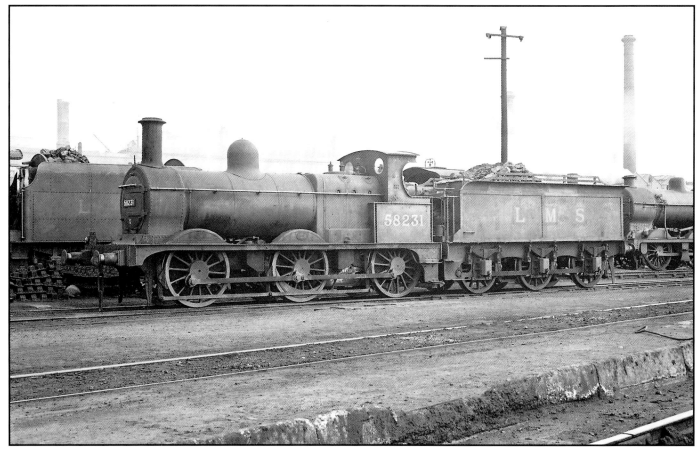

22) It is a remarkable fact that for many years the Midland Railway moved huge tonnages of coal with diminutive locomotives such as 2F Class 0-6-0 No 58231 (ex. LMS No 3138). This Johnson engine with four foot eleven inches driving wheels is of 1885 vintage and was one of twenty-one examples to come into British Railways ownership and is seen in a less than pristine condition in the yard of its home shed at 21A Saltley on 13th August 1949. (A.N.H.Glover)

23) Soon to become yet another withdrawal statistic, LMS Class 2 2-6-0 No 46475, locally based at 67E Dumfries, comes off the Castle Douglas line with a mixed freight and heads for Dumfries station on 5th June 1964. For many years a North Eastern Region locomotive (51A Darlington and 52D Tweedmouth), No 46475 had made its way to Dumfries shed in November 1963. Withdrawn in July 1964 it was scrapped at the West of Scotland Shipbreaking Co., Troon. (D.K.Jones)

24) Newly allocated to 9B Stockport from 12A Carlisle (Upperby), LMS Fowler Class 4 2-6-4T No 42343 has been smartly turned out as it steams along at Guide Bridge with a Leeds to Stockport train consisting of a couple of vans and three passenger coaches on a bright 20th June 1957. Remaining at 9B for a number of years, No 42343 left for good in May 1965 finding a new home at 8F Springs Branch Wigan. Its final base was at 9E Trafford Park. (B.K.B.Green)

25) With the driver looking forwards from the cab of his charge, LMS Fowler Class 4 2-6-4T No 42359, from 11B Barrow, arrives at Lancaster Castle station with a local passenger train on a sun-filled day in 1955. In October 1957, No 42359 was despatched south to London and to a new home at 1A Willesden. In June of the following year it moved across London to 14D Neasden, but three months later it was back at 1A. Withdrawal came in October 1964. (N.E.Preedy)

26) The twin cooling towers of a power station dominate the flat landscape near to Agecroft Junction in the fifties. Having passed the compact signalbox, LMS Class 4 2-6-4T No 42484 lifts its safety valves as it approaches the camera with a four-coach local passenger working. Note the 'open' catchpoints in the foreground. There used to be a station at Agecroft but it had closed as far back as 1861. No 42484 was withdrawn 105 years later in January 1966. (B.K.B.Green)

27) A gloomy day at Dalry Road in Edinburgh in 1959. In steam alongside the four-road running shed is locally based LMS Class 5 4-6-0 No 45023 which is in the company of an unidentified ex. North British Railway J37 Class 0-6-0. Constructed by the Caledonian Railway, Dalry Road shed was coded 28B from 1948 to 1949 and 64C from then onwards until complete closure on 3rd October 1965, two years after No 45023 had been withdrawn from service. (Mike Higson)

28) A splendid view of the former London & North Western Railway four-road shed at Oxenholme, coded 11D, 11C and 12G under British Railways. Its main duties were to supply banking engines for the northbound workings up Grayrigg bank. After closure on 18th August 1962 its allocation of locomotives and shed staff were transferred to Carnforth. In front of the shed on 13th August 1950 are LMS Class 4 2-6-4 Tanks Nos 42313 and 42464. (B.K.B.Green)

29) Bletchley depot was situated on the west side of the main line to the north of the station and had a large and varied allocation over the years. This was another shed which changed codes from time to time under BR - 2B (1948-1950), 4A (1950-1952) and finally 1E up until closure on 5th July 1965. In steam and receiving attention to its motion on 30th May 1964 is LMS Class 8F 2-8-0 No 48207, for many years an inhabitant of Bletchley shed. (D.K.Jones)

30) The Fowler versions of the LMS Class 4 2-6-4 Tanks were easily distinguishable from the other members of the class with their parallel boilers and were the first to be introduced into traffic in 1927. Along with the Fairburn and Stanier versions a total of 645 were eventually built. On station pilot duties in the sidings at Leicester (Midland) station in the fifties is a local steed, No 42330 which was withdrawn in December 1961. (R.S.Carpenter)

31) Looking the worse for wear, McIntosh Caledonian Railway Class 2P 0-4-4T No 55196 is photographed on duty inside Oban station on a sunny October day in 1952. No 55196 is based at the near-at-hand shed, 63E, once owned by the Eastern Region of BR and coded 31C from 1948-1949. By January 1957 only fifty-one of these engines were still in service. No 55196 was withdrawn during the fifties and the class was rendered extinct by December 1962. (R.Butterfield)

32) The London Midland and Scottish Railway in its wisdom added 195 more members of the LMS Class 4P Compound 4-4-0's to its stock between the years 1924 and 1932, originally for top link express duties. By 25th May 1953, No 41154 (9E Trafford Park) was less strenuously employed when recorded at Marple station, on the Derby-Manchester main line, on a stopping passenger train. The long and ornately designed footbridge is worthy of note. (B.K.B.Green)

33) LMS Class 2P 0-4-4T No 41902 is a visitor to 3B Bushbury (Wolverhampton) from 3C Walsall as it stands outside the straight running shed on 1st January 1956. Bushbury shed, later coded 21C and 2K, was one of the last depots on the London Midland Region to house examples of the former LNWR Class 7F 0-8-0's, closing its doors to steam on 10th April 1965. No 41902, later based at 2C Warwick and 2A Rugby, succumbed to withdrawal in November 1959. (B.K.B.Green)

34) The motive power depot at 1A Willesden was a massive affair with a large allocation and consisted of a roundhouse and a straight shed and for the spotter on foot it was only a five minute walk from Willesden Junction station. On the occasion of the author's last visit on 1st March 1964 there were seventy-eight steam engines to be seen. On 15th July 1952, LMS Caprotti Class 5 4-6-0 No 44686, from 9A Longsight, is in steam in the yard. (B.K.B.Green)

35) An unwelcome diesel locomotive intrudes into this photograph taken on a summer's day at Carlisle (Citadel) on 4th July 1964. Awaiting departure to the south is the 10.35am Glasgow to Blackpool and Southport express which is double-headed by LMS Class 5 4-6-0 No 44971 (6B Mold Junction) and BR *Britannia* Class 4-6-2 No 70011 *Hotspur*, locally based at 12A Kingmoor. The latter engine survived at 12A until the shed closed at the end of 1967. (D.K.Jones)

36) The former Caledonian Railway terminus at Glasgow (Buchanan Street) often hosted ex. London & North Eastern Railway passenger locomotives, particularly between 1962 and 1965 on the three hour trains from Glasgow to Aberdeen. Coasting into Buchanan Street at the end of its journey from Aberdeen on a wet June day in 1963 is LNER A2 Class 4-6-2 No 60527 *Sun Chariot*, from 61B Aberdeen (Ferryhill). It was transferred to 66A Polmadie in October 1963. (R.W.Hinton)

37) The large straight running shed at 5D Stoke was an open-ended affair situated in cramped surroundings. Standing outside one end of the depot in May 1962 are two unidentified LMS Class 3F 0-6-0 Tanks. In the right of the frame, attempting to hide behind heaps of discarded ash, is locally based LMS Class 6P5F 'Crab' 2-6-0 No 42889 which was withdrawn during this same month. To the rear of No 42889 is sister engine No 42772, of 6C Birkenhead. (N.E.Preedy)

38) Two pairs of identical locomotives are on show at 9B Stockport on 3rd May 1952. In the distance are two LMS Class 6P5F 2-6-0's in steam and nearer to the camera we can identify two LMS Fowler Class 4 2-6-4 Tanks, Nos 42332 and 42352. No 42332 ended its days at 12E Barrow being condemned in October 1961. No 42352 lasted a few months longer, withdrawn from 15C Leicester (Midland) in May 1962. Both locomotives were scrapped at Derby Works. (B.K.B.Green)

39) The 23rd December 1962 heralded the beginning of the 'Big Freeze' during the winter of 1962/63. On the day after it all started there is a sprinkling of snow on the ground as LMS Class 8F 2-8-0 No 48747, from 21B Bescot, passes Wednesbury under partially clear signals and heads for Dudley with a mixed freight. Once a longstanding resident of 8C Speke Junction (until June 1962), No 48747 survived in service until September 1966. (T.R.Amos)

40) McIntosh designed four famous classes of 4-4-0's for the Caledonian Railway between 1895 and 1910. The first example was named *Dunalastair* from the estate of that name owned by the Company Chairman. The last class to be built was known as *Dunalastair IV* and the engines had large double-bogie tenders. No 14363 is seen here eking out its last days of service on shunting duties near to the station at Aviemore on 9th June 1948. (W.Boydon)

41) Of Great Northern Railway heritage the branch line from Luton to Dunstable (Town) came under the ownership of the LMR until it was closed under the 'Beeching Axe' in 1965 and on 29th June 1953 weeds are beginning to sprout in the siding in the left of the frame. In Dunstable (Town) on local passenger trains are LNER N7/5 Class 0-6-2T No 69648 and LMS Class 4 2-6-4T No 42591. Of these two engines, No 42591 survived the longest being withdrawn in October 1962. (B.K.B.Green)

42) A dilapidated building forms a backdrop for this photograph taken in the shed yard at 16A Nottingham on 22nd June 1952, Facing the camera is LMS Fowler Class 4 2-6-4T No 42331 which is a visitor to Nottingham shed from 15C Leicester (Midland). The locomotive behind No 42331 is an LNER J39 Class 0-6-0. No 42331 was withdrawn from 15C in August 1962 and stored there until around April 1963, being sent for scrap to Cashmores, Great Bridge. (B.K.B.Green)

43) On the first day of nationalisation British Railways inherited fourteen of the diminutive McIntosh Caledonian Class 0F 0-4-0 Saddle Tanks, some of which were employed at Crewe and St.Rollox Works on a semi-permanent basis. Proudly displaying the lettering of its new owner, No 56025 poses by some driving wheels in the yard at St.Rollox Works on 5th June 1949. Withdrawn in May 1960, No 56025 was rather ironically cut up at Inverurie Works. (A.N.H.Glover)

25

44) Large lumps of coal litter the ground near to the coaling plant at 10F Rose Grove in July 1968 where a respectable looking LMS Class 8F 2-8-0 No 48730 simmers gently as it contemplates what little is left of its life. This locomotive spent much of its career in South Wales, being allocated to 87K Swansea (Victoria) and 87F Llanelly. It departed from the Western Region in September 1964 serving at 10D Lostock Hall before moving on to Rose Grove. (C.P.Stacey)

45) The grim building in the background with its 'horror film' style of Victorian chimneys is part of the station scene at Earlstown on a wet 5th February 1966. A what is now an old fashioned perambulator peeps out from behind one of two coaches which form a Locomotive Club of Great Britain special being hauled by LMS Class 2 2-6-2T No 41286, from 8G Sutton Oak, a depot it was to die at after being condemned in November 1966. (B.K.B.Green)

46) A dismal February day in 1957 finds LMS Class 6P5F 2-6-0 No 42781 in steam in the yard of its home depot at 2B Nuneaton. This shed, of London & North Western Railway origin, was situated between the West Coast Main Line and the route to Coventry. It consisted of eight roads with an extensive yard. No 42781 took its leave of 2B in September 1961, moving to 5A Crewe (North). A transfer in May 1962 took it to its last home at 6A Chester. (N.E.Preedy)

47) For many years up the closure of the former Great Central Railway two-road shed at 6F Bidston in February 1963 it had a numerical trio of BR Class 9F 2-10-0's on its books, Nos 92045-47. In June 1962, No 92046 is noted in the yard at 6F with a sister engine. Upon closure all three were transferred to 6C Birkenhead, being withdrawn between September and November 1967. One 'oddity' based at 6F was WD Class 8F 2-10-0 No 90763. (Ray Harris)

48) The former Midland Railway shed at Westhouses, coded 18B and 16G under BR, was situated adjacent to Blackwell Sidings and Blackwell South Junction, a five minute walk from Westhouses and Blackwell station, closed in 1967. Its prime function was the movement of coal traffic from Blackwell Colliery, presumably now long gone. In the summer of 1960 one of Westhouses inmates, LMS Class 3F 'Jinty' No 47250, is seen at rest in the shed yard. (B.K.B.Green)

49) The ten units of the 41900-9 series of LMS Class 2P 0-4-4 Tanks were designed by Stanier and first came into service in 1932 equipped with push and pull apparatus. On 8th August 1953, No 41903 is in a peaceful setting 'under the wires' at Lancaster (Castle) station with a local passenger train. No 41903 is one of two such engines based at 11E Lancaster (Green Ayre), the other being No 41904. Both were withdrawn in November 1959. (B.K.B.Green)

50) Yet another numerical coincidence, this time concerning BR Class 5 4-6-0 No 73055 seen at rest between duties at Glasgow (Central) in May 1959. At this stage in time Nos 73055-64 were all allocated to 66A Polmadie (Glasgow) where all but three examples, Nos 73056-58, were to remain until taken out of service, the latter engines being transferred away in June and July 1964. No 73055, withdrawn in June 1966, was scrapped at McLellans, Langloan. (N.E.Preedy)

51) The value of smoke deflectors is clear for all to see as BR *Britannia* Class 4-6-2 No 70020 *Mercury* tracks along beneath overhead wires at Ashton, near Roade, in deep shadows with an express freight on 9th June 1964. *Mercury*, in deplorable external condition, is an inmate of 1A Willesden. Once of 86C Cardiff (Canton) it was transferred to the LMR in September 1961. *Mercur*y was withdrawn from 12A Carlisle (Kingmoor) in January 1967. (Terry Ward)

52) With a decrepit building in the left of the frame a rather mangy looking former Midland Railway Class 0F 0-4-0T No 41529 is on show at Staveley on 8th July 1953. Designed by Deeley in 1907, two examples of the class, Nos 41528 and 41533, survived well beyond their 'sell-by date' and were not withdrawn until December 1966. No 41529 managed to linger on at 41E Staveley (Barrow Hill) until April 1961, being scrapped at Derby Works two months later. (B.K.B.Green)

53) With the bridge carrying the main road from Edinburgh (A90) in the right background, the massive concrete coaling plant at the former Caledonian Railway shed at 63A Perth dominates the scene. In steam in front of the plant on 2nd April 1961 is LNER A3 Class 4-6-2 No 60096 *Papyrus*, from 64B Haymarket and sporting a partially scorched smokebox. *Papyrus*, modified with a double chimney in July 1958, later received German smoke deflectors. (D.K.Jones)

54) The flat landscape at Manchester (London Road) is punctuated by the massive station roof, an elevated structure that appears to be akin to a POW 'watchtower', and a large water tank as an immaculate looking LMS Fowler Class 4 2-6-4T No 42371 (9D Buxton) accelerates away with a local passenger train on a sunny 26th February 1953. No 42371 was destined to remain in revenue earning service at Buxton shed until May 1962, being scrapped at Crewe Works. (B.K.B.Green)

55) Taking advantage of a weed-strewn hummock, the photographer is perfectly positioned to capture on camera the passing of LMS Class 4F 'Duck Six' No 44236 (21A Saltley) as it rattles through a deserted Coleshill station (closed in 1968) on the outskirts of Birmingham with a Washwood Heath freight in the mid-fifties. Later in the fifties, No 44236 was transferred to Manchester at 9F Heaton Mersey and in December 1959 it was drafted to 9G Gorton. (R.S.Carpenter).

56) Looking fresh from what was probably its last overhaul, LMS Class 8F 2-8-0 No 48171 is seen in steam in the yard of its home shed at the bleak outpost of 9L Buxton on 10th April 1966 in the company of a sister engine. Allocated to 1A Willesden for many years, No 48171 was subjected to four transfers during 1965, these being at 5B Crewe - South (January), 5D Stoke (February), 9D Newton Heath (August) and finally to Buxton shed (October). (C.P.Stacey)

57) Fitted with equipment for working auto-trains and in a highly presentable condition, home-based LMR Class 2 2-6-2T No 41271 releases steam from its cylinder cocks in the yard at 15D Bedford in the company of an unidentified LMS Class 8F 2-8-0 in February 1957. Bedford shed, a four-road structure, situated between Bedford North and Kempston Road Junctions, closed to steam in September 1963, twelve months after No 41271 was withdrawn. (N.E.Preedy)

58) Passengers throng the platform at Lowton St.Marys station for the first time for many months on 22nd May 1965 after the closure of the same during 1964. The focus of attention is on spruced-up LMS Class 4 2-6-4T No 42587, from 8F Springs Branch Wigan, which is in charge of a Railway Correspondence and Travel Society special. Once of 14B Kentish Town, 14C St.Albans, 17A Derby, 16A Nottingham and 16B Kirkby, No 42587 had been at 8F since November 1964. (B.K.B.Green)

59) A member of the footplate crew of Pickersgill Caledonian Class 3P 4-4-0 No 54482, minus shedplate but allocated to 60E Forres, takes things easy as his charge simmers and sizzles in Georgemas Junction station in the far north of Scotland with a freight in the summer of 1956. No 54482 was transferred to 60B Aviemore in March 1957 where it worked until withdrawal in February 1962 eventually being cut up in a scrapyard in Troon. (N.E.Preedy)

60) The LMS Class 2P 4-4-0's were first introduced in 1928 and were a post-grouping development of an earler Midland Railway design. On a dull 29th June 1957, smartly turned out No 40685, based at 24H Hellifield, storms through Long Preston station, situated between Hellifield and Skipton, with an excursion (M603). Condemned from 24H in July 1961 it lay rusting there until summoned to Horwich Works for scrapping in December 1962. (B.K.B.Green)

61) Bright sunshine envelopes the busy scene in the yard at 1A Willesden in April 1962. In the background are two LMS Class 5 4-6-0's, a BR *Britannia* Class 4-6-2 and LMS Class 8F 2-8-0 No 48551, a Willesden locomotive. Nearest the camera is LMS *Royal Scot* Class 4-6-0 No 46110 *Grenadier Guardsman*, from 8A Edge Hill (Liverpool). Rendered redundant from Edge Hill depot in June 1963, *Grenadier Guardsman* was drafted to 12A Carlisle (Kingmoor). (Ray Harris)

62) Engines abound in the works yard at Horwich on 7th October. Facing us are two engines which are fresh from repair, LMS Class 4F 'Duck Six' 0-6-0 No 44339 and LMS Class 7F 0-8-0 No 49598. Elsewhere in the yard is former Lancashire & Yorkshire Class 2F 0-6-2ST No 51429. No 49598 (27D Wigan L & Y) was the first to be withdrawn in January 1959. This was followed by No 51429, from Horwich, in May 1961 and No 44339 in December 1965 (9L Buxton). (B.K.B.Green)

63) An unusual portrait as taken at 9F Heaton Mersey on 23rd February 1967 where a member of the shed staff and another gentleman are engaged in conversation. Note the Cheshire Lines Committee cast-iron plate on the wall. In the left of the frame in steam is LMS Class 8F 2-8-0 No 48168, a local engine, and LMS Class 5 4-6-0 No 44679, from 8F Springs Branch Wigan. Upon the closure of Heaton Mersey in May 1968, No 48168 was posted to 9K Bolton. (M.S.Stokes)

64) The wide cutting at Heaton Moor contains four tracks and a platelayers hut and the peace and quiet is temporarily suspended as LMS Class 4F 0-6-0 No 44075 trundles along at the head of a lengthy freight train on 24th May 1953. Records show us that No 44075 was allocated to 9B Stockport by January 1957, a depot it was to serve at twice before withdrawal in November 1965. It also worked from 5E Alsager, 6H Bangor, 2E Northampton and 8G Sutton Oak. (B.K.B.Green)

65) By the end of April 1960 the amount of short distance goods traffic in the Scottish lowlands was much reduced from former times and there was little need for the legions of ex. Caledonian Railway 'Jumbo' Class 0-6-0's like No 57236. Constructed in 1884 at a cost of £2900, No 57236 (67B Hurlford) lies rusting in store on a dead road at 67A Corkerhill (Glasgow). Although not withdrawn until September 1961, it is doubtful if it ever worked again. (Peter Hay)

66) Although it is the 9th September 1962, 5C Stafford based LMS Class 3F 0-6-0T No 47649 is still sporting the small 'lion-on-wheel' emblem of British Railways in the yard at 17A Derby. For many years a common sight in the freight yards at Stafford on shunting duties, No 47649 was transferred to 5F Uttoxeter in August 1964. When the latter closed in December 1964, No 47649 moved to 5D Stoke. It ended its days as a shunter at Crewe Works. (T.R.Amos)

67) The Deeley designed (1906) Midland Railway Class 3F 0-6-0's were rebuilt later in life with a Belpaire firebox and one example (No 43808) survived until September 1962. No 43825 is seen here in the yard of its home shed at 18A Toton on 13th May 1956, not long before being transferred to 18B Westhouses. It remained at 18B until November 1961, moving on to 17C Rowsley. Condemned in April 1962 it was scrapped at Derby Works a month later. (B.K.B.Green)

68) With the tall chimneys of the Manchester skyline in the background veiled in a hazy atmosphere, the sun's rays reflect off the front end of LMS Class 2P 4-4-0 No 40538 as it passes the compact signalbox and arrives at an apparently deserted Heaton Mersey station with a local passenger train on 24th July 1953. By January 1957, No 40538 was allocated to 19B Millhouses, but in October of the same year it moved to its last abode at 17A Derby. (B.K.B.Green)

69) Closed during 1962 nature is beginning to claim the platforms at Strathbungo station (Glasgow) in June 1964. The enclosed footbridge is still in situ at Strathbungo as 12A Carlisle (Kingmoor) allocated BR *Britannia* Class 4-6-2 No 70041 *Sir John Moore* passes by with an early evening stopper bound for Carlisle. Once of 30A Stratford, 32A Norwich and 40B Immingham, No 70041 was drafted to the LMR at 12B Carlisle (Upperby) in December 1963. (R.W.Hinton)

70) A close-up of one of the inhabitants of the former Midland Railway depot at Burton on 8th July 1951. LMS Class 2P 4-4-0 No 40526 stands over an ash disposal pit in the company of an unidentified 0-6-0 type. Burton shed, coded 17B and 16F in BR days, consisted of two covered roundhouses and a large yard. In 1950 it housed a most unusual occupant, Class 0F 0-4-0ST No 56020 of The Caledonian Railway. Burton closed in September 1966 to steam. (B.K.B.Green)

71) Possibly substituting for an English Electric Type 4 main line diesel, LMS *Royal Scot* Class 4-6-0 No 46155 *The Lancer*, from 5A Crewe (North), speeds through Bletchley station, some forty-seven miles from Euston, with a down express bound for Holyhead on a dark September day in 1963. From June 1958 up until withdrawal in December 1964, *The Lancer* was also based at 8A Edge Hill, 1B Camden, 6G Llandudno Junction and 12A Carlisle (Kingmoor). (I.J.Hodson)

72) By 1963 Western Region territory in the West Midlands was firmly in the hands of the LMR authorities, though the former retained the WR influence in terms of general infrastructure and attitudes for some years to come. One area that was gradually eroded was the motive power element and former GWR engines were gradually replaced by LMS ones, though the one seen at Banbury on 14th September 1965 is a visitor from 16F Burton, Class 8F 2-8-0 No 48681. (D.K.Jones)

73) Following the severe fire at 24K Preston in June 1961, the roofless shed was cleaned up and used for the storage of redundant and withdrawn steam locomotives for some considerable time afterwards. Photographed inside the 'cleaned up' depot in June 1962 are two stored LMS Unrebuilt *Patriot* Class 4-6-0's Nos 45533 *Lord Rathmore* (8A Edge Hill) and 45549, withdrawn from 8B Warrington during the same month this picture was taken. (Ray Harris)

74) The running shed at 66A Polmadie (Glasgow) was a massive affair with an immense yard and was a pleasure to visit in steam days. In the company of a BR Class 4 2-6-2T, LMS Class 5 4-6-0 No 45011 (66E Carstairs) is fresh from overhaul in May 1960. To the right of No 45011 is LMS *Coronation* Class 4-6-2 No 46240 *City of Coventry*, from 1B Camden, which is awaiting its next duty back to London. No 45011 was withdrawn in December 1965 from 66E. (N.E.Preedy)

75) With a Class 2 2-6-0 type lurking in the right of this picture, 25D Mirfield based Hughes LMS Class 6P5F 2-6-0 No 42861, in quite atrocious external condition, steams beneath a large signal gantry as it draws into Manchester (Victoria) with an excursion on 5th March 1955. Based at 56A Wakefield in later years, No 42861 moved to Scotland in November 1963 to 67B Hurlford (Kilmarnock). It ended its days in July 1966 from 67C Ayr. (B.K.B.Green)

76) The external condition of LMS *Royal Scot* Class 4-6-0 No 46140 *The King's Royal Rifle Corps* is on about the same par as No 42861 in the previous photograph. 26A Newton Heath based, No 46140 is coasting along light engine at Aylesbury on 15th June 1963. Transferred to 9A Longsight (Manchester) during this same month, No 46140 remained there until October 1964, moving to 12A Carlisle (Kingmoor) where it was destined to die in November 1965. (D.K.Jones)

77) This is yet another locomotive which looks in dire need of the cleaners attention. With an unidentified LMS Class 5 4-6-0 in the left of the frame, LMS Class 4 2-6-0 No 43012 parades its ugly double chimney in the shed yard at 17A Derby on 16th August 1953. This chimney was later replaced with a single one. During its last years of life, No 43012 worked from 15B Kettering, 21B Bournville, 21A Saltley, 15A Wellingborough, 9F Heaton Mersey and 52F Blyth. (B.K.B.Green)

78) Once the 'jewel in the crown' of the Western Region in the Midlands, Birmingham (Snow Hill), by 24th April 1965, was firmly in the grip of the London Midland Region. This Stephenson Locomotive Special, bound for the North Warwick line and beyond, is hauled by a 'compromise' duet. The leading engine is LMS Class 4F 0-6-0 No 44188, from 2F Bescot. The train engine is GWR 6400 Class 0-6-0PT No 6435, withdrawn in October 1964 for preservation. (B.K.B.Green)

79) With a range of mountains in the background the station at Killin looks little more than a glorified 'bus shelter' and is sparsely populated in the summer of 1963. Simmering in the station is BR Class 4 2-6-4T No 80092 (Perth), which has not long arrived from Killin Junction. This branch line was doomed to closure in 1965. No 80092, once of 6H Bangor and 6A Chester, was condemned from 63A in September 1966 and scrapped at Campbells, Airdrie. (R.S.Carpenter)

80) Despite the massive influx of English Electric Type 4 main line diesels on the West Coast Main Line by 11th August 1964, the job of standby engine at 1E Bletchley for the Royal Train was entrusted to twenty-four year old LMS *Coronation* Class 4-6-2 No 46240 *City of Coventry* (1A Willesden) which is on parade at 1E in superb external condition. Later in the month of August *City of Coventry* was transferred to a final home at 5A Crewe (North). (C.P.Stacey)

81) In direct contrast to *City of Coventry* in the previous picture, LMS *Jubilee* Class 4-6-0 No 45596 *Bahamas*, from 9B Stockport and equipped with a double chimney, is in a filthy state in the yard at 1E Northampton on 22nd July 1964. For many years on the books at 8A Edge Hill (Liverpool), *Bahamas* had a brief spell at 12B Carlisle (Upperby) before arriving at 9B in July 1962. Withdrawn in July 1966 it is now actively preserved. (Terry Ward)

82) Black smoke pours from the funnel of LMS Class 5 4-6-0 No 44754, from 20A Leeds (Holbeck), as it bears down on the photographer at speed with a partially fitted freight at Hellifield on 24th March 1951. This is a Caprotti valve geared locomotive, introduced in 1948, and the large outside steampipes gives it an ungainly appearance. It remained at Holbeck shed until September 1964, moving firstly to 9B Stockport and then to 8C Speke Junction. (B.K.B.Green)

83) Former Midland Railway Class 3F 0-6-0 No 43329, an 8B Warrington steed, pulls out of Manchester (London Road) with a local passenger train on 20th March 1957. Waiting in the left background is BR *Britannia* Class 4-6-2 No 70044 *Earl Haig*, from 9A Longsight (Manchester), which is in charge of *The Mancunian*, complete with appropriate headboard. No 43329 moved to 9D Buxton in October 1957 where it remained in service until June 1960. (B.K.B.Green)

84) In the early sixties a 'dump' for redundant steam engines was created at Lugton, halfway between Glasgow and Kilmarnock. On an unknown date in 1962 several locomotives lie dead and rusting in the sidings. From left to right we can identify ex. Caledonian Railway Class 2P 0-4-4 Tanks Nos 55266 and 55206, which had both been withdrawn in September 1961. In the extreme right of the frame is LMS *Jubilee* Class 4-6-0 No 45665 *Lord Rutherford of Nelson*. (R.Butterfield)

85) Bright sunshine outside 12A Carlisle (Kingmoor) shed in July 1958 where LMS Class 6P5F 'Crab' 2-6-0 No 42814 is a visitor to the depot from 9A Longsight. No 42814, transferred to 6C Birkenhead in November 1960, is flanked by LMS *Royal Scot* Class 4-6-0 No 46167 *The Hertfordshire Regiment*, from 12B Carlisle (Upperby) and LMS *Jubilee* Class 4-6-0 No 45672 *Anson*, of 1B Camden. No 42814 was withdrawn from Birkenhead in August 1965. (N.E.Preedy)

86) A rarely photographed shed on the London Midland Region was at Wigan L & Y which was coded 23D, 27D and 8P under British Railways. Having once had fourteen roads, BR reduced it to eight of which only two eventually remained covered. With the 'luxurious' staff quarters in the left of the picture, resident LMS Class 4F 0-6-0 No 44225 is noted in steam in the yard on 18th August 1957. This locomotive was withdrawn from the shed in November 1959. (B.K.B.Green)

87) Dark smoke from the double chimney of begrimed LMS Class 4 'Flying Pig' 2-6-0 No 43041 blackens the overhead electric wires at Thurlstone on 6th April 1953. No 43041 is in charge of the 9.47am excursion from Heeley to Hyde Road. In common with the other members of the class which were fitted with double chimneys, No 43041 later acquired the more conventional single one. It finished its career allocated to 10D Lower Darwen. (B.K.B.Green)

88) Looking in need of a good clean, BR *Britannia* Class 4-6-2 No 70009 *Alfred the Great*, from 12A Carlisle (Kingmoor), takes on water at Stirling station whilst in charge of a down empty coaching stock train on a wet Friday 13th November 1964. *Alfred the Great*, once a long-term resident of 32A Norwich, moved to 31B March in September 1961. No 70009 left the Eastern Region for Carlisle in December 1963, in common with the other 31B *Britannias*. (A.C.Ingram)

89) In fine external condition, 25D Mirfield allocated LMS Class 4F 0-6-0 No 44062 passes Luddendenfoot station, of Lancashire & Yorkshire Railway origin, with a lengthy goods train on 12th May 1956. At the end of 1956, the likes of Mirfield, Wakefield, Low Moor etc., passed into the hands of the North Eastern Region authorities, as did No 44062 for the remainder of its working life. It was condemned from 56A Wakefield in September 1962. (B.K.B.Green)

90) A numerical batch of BR Caprotti Class 5 4-6-0's were allocated to 65B St.Rollox from new, between January and June 1957, these being Nos 73145-54 and all but a few spent their short working lives at this shed. In August 1960, No 73153 stands in the yard at 65B with a sister engine. No 73153 was transferred to 65J Stirling in November 1966, but this was only a brief stay of execution, being condemned from there during the following month. (N.E.Preedy)

91) It was nothing unusual to discover over 150 steam locomotives on Birmingham's Saltley shed (21A) on Sundays in the late forties including a large complement of former Midland Railway 0-6-0's. This example, No 3052, has an extended cab for better protection from the weather and is noted out of steam outside a roofless roundhouse on 13th August 1949. Keeping No 3052 company is LMS Class 1F 0-6-0T No 41879 which ended up at 82E Bristol Barrow Road. (A.N.H.Glover)

92) LMS Class 4P Compound 4-4-0 No 40925 lets off steam as it departs from an all but deserted Manchester (Exchange) station with an unidentified express on 17th March 1954. This large station of London & North Western Railway origin closed in 1969. No 40925 worked from 6G Llandudno Junction, 9A Longsight (Manchester), 21B Bournville and 17A Derby during the latter stages of its life and was condemned from Derby shed in November 1959. (B.K.B.Green)

93) Having escaped the wholesale withdrawals earlier in the month, LMS Rebuilt *Patriot* Class 4-6-0 No 45522 *Prestatyn*, from 26A Newton Heath, is seen in filthy condition on the downgrade at Shap with an express on 22nd September 1962. Note the catchpoints to the left of *Prestatyn*. In September 1963 No 45522 was transferred to 9A Longsight (Manchester) where it was to survive until September 1964, after which it was stored at 9L Buxton. (R.Picton)

94) A general view of the yard and depot at Kirkby-in-Ashfield in September 1965. The original three-road shed is on the left and on the right is a two-road structure which was added in 1958. In front of the depot are several LMS Class 8F 2-8-0's, including Nos 48219, a visitor from 15E Coalville, and 48405 a local inmate. Coded 16C (1948-1955), 16B (1955 to September 1963) and 16E onwards, Kirkby-in-Ashfield closed to steam on 3rd October 1966. (N.E.Preedy)

95) A trio of LMS Class 5 4-6-0's are parked in steam near to the turntable and the half-roundhouse at 5A Crewe (North) on 18th March 1962. Nearest the camera is No 44687, of 6G Llandudno Junction, which was built in 1951 with Caprotti valve gear and Skefco roller bearings. A once longstanding resident of 9A Longsight (Manchester), No 44687 was drafted to 8M Southport from Llandudno Junction in October 1963 and was withdrawn in January 1966. (J.M.Tolson)

96) This close-up of LMS Class 5 4-6-0 No 44669, from 12A Carlisle (Kingmoor), shows it at rest in platform 3 at Glasgow (Central) station in August 1965. The letters SC beneath the shedplate indicate it has a self-cleaning smokebox, the door having a single lamp bracket between the hinges. Along the footplating beside the cab is the AWS reservoir, the contact shoe itself being protected from a swinging front coupling by a metal plate. (N.E.Preedy)

97) The photographer is hiding amidst shrubbery at Uppingham station as passengers from a Railway Correspondence and Travel Society special mill around on 18th May 1963. This small station, terminus of a short branch line, had closed to normal traffic in 1960. Standing near to the buffers at Uppingham is LMS Class 4 2-6-4T No 42087, from 15C Leicester (Midland), which later worked from the sheds at 9K Bolton, 9D Newton Heath and 8H Birkenhead. (D.Webster)

98) A warm looking spring day at Chinley on 17th May 1952 with trees loaded with blossom. Despite what appears to be a supreme effort, LMS Class 4F 0-6-0 No 43963 in the right of the frame on a freight train is overtaken by a smartly turned out LMS Class 4P Compound 4-4-0 No 41159, of 9A Longsight (Manchester), which is in charge of a lengthy local passenger working. Withdrawn in April 1958, No 41159 was stored at Badnalls Wharf, Norton Bridge. (B.K.B.Green)

99) With a sister locomotive at the rear and with a BR *Clan* Class 4-6-2 for company, LMS Fowler Class 4 2-6-4T No 42417, with a side-window cab, poses for the camera in front of the running shed at 66A Polmadie (Glasgow) on a dull 3rd August 1952. Based at 66D Greenock (Ladyburn), No 42417 had found its way to 6D Chester (Northgate) by January 1957. Its last home was at Saltley between August 1960 and April 1964, after which it was cut up at Crewe. (B.K.B.Green)

100) Photographed in fine external condition, but bereft of shedplate, ex. Midland Railway Class 3F 0-6-0 No 43342 is hemmed between a sister engine and a BR Class 9F 2-10-0 in a siding alongside its home shed at 17C Rowsley on a sunny 28th February 1960. No 43342 remained at 17C until December 1962, moving briefy to 14E Bedford. Between January 1963 and withdrawal eight months later, No 43342 rotated between the sheds at Derby and Bedford again. (B.K.B.Green)

101) Totally neglected by the cleaning staff at its home shed at 5A Crewe (North), LMS *Coronation* Class 4-6-2 No 46228 *Duchess of Rutland* takes refreshment from a water column near to the coaling plant in the yard at 1A Willesden on a dark Sunday morning on 28th June 1964 before running light engine to Euston to head a northbound excursion (1Z35). Within less than four months the fires on this fine locomotive will have been drawn for the last time. (M.S.Stokes)

102) For many years an inhabitant of 2A Rugby, begrimed LMS Class 5 4-6-0 No 44915 heads through Rugby (Midland) with a rake of coaching stock on 8th April 1963. In January 1963, No 44915 was rendered surplus to operating requirements at Rugby shed and transferred to 1E Bletchley where it remained until July of the same year, moving to a final abode at 10D Lostock Hall (Preston). Condemned in December 1967 it was scrapped at Wards, Beighton. (D.K.Jones)

103) With the front end of an LMS Class 3F 'Jinty' 0-6-0T peeping out of the covered section of the roundhouse at 12B Carlisle (Upperby) on 12th October 1963, 5A Crewe (North) allocated BR *Britannia* Class 4-6-2 No 70025 *Western Star* releases steam from its cylinder cocks whilst standing on the turntable. Once of 86C Cardiff (Canton) and 21D Aston, *Western Star* was also shedded at 5B Crewe (South), 6G Llandudno Junction and 12A Carlisle (Kingmoor). (D.K.Jones)

104) Following an overhaul at the nearby works, newly painted and lined-out LMS Fowler Class 4 2-6-4T No 42415 waits in the yard at 17A Derby to be steamed again and returned home to 6H Bangor on 13th May 1956. Between June 1957 and withdrawal in December 1962, No 42415 was employed at 6D Chester (Northgate), 9B Stockport, 21A Saltley, 15C Leicester (Midland), 12E Barrow, 24L Carnforth and 12H Tebay. It was scrapped at Crewe Works in July 1963. (B.K.B.Green)

105) Former Caledonian Railway *Dunalastair IV* Class 3P No 54439, built in 1907 and rebuilt in 1915, is seen fully coaled and in light steam outside the compact brick-built two-road shed at 60D Wick in the early fifties not too many years before withdrawal from active service. Wick shed, originally owned by the Highland Railway, had the privilege of housing the last three HR *Ben* Class 4-4-0's, Nos 54398 *Ben Alder*, 54399 *Ben Wyvis* and 54404 *Ben Clebrig*. (R.Butterfield)

106) LMS *Coronation* Class 4-6-2 No 46227 *Duchess of Devonshire*, a longstanding inmate at 66A Polmadie (Glasgow), is reduced to powering a local passenger train, seen here departing from Carlisle (Citadel) station on a wet 27th September 1962. Condemned from 66A three months later, this 1938 built Pacific was stored there until May 1963 and then at 65C Parkhead prior to being called to Crewe Works for scrapping in November 1963. (R.Picton)

107) LMS Class 4F 0-6-0 No 44336 departs from Newton Heath station with a clear road ahead whilst heading a local passenger train consisting of a rake of elderly carriages on 4th May 1952. One wonders how many spotters alighted at this station to take the five-minute walk to Newton Heath shed which is out of sight, but near at hand. However, from 1966 onwards the spotters would have had to make alternative arrangements after the station was closed. (B.K.B.Green)

108) A quiet scene at 12A Carlisle (Kingmoor) as two residents of the depot simmer in front of the running shed in the summer of 1964. Nearest the camera is BR *Clan* Class 4-6-2 No 72005 *Clan Macgregor* which was constructed in 1952 and withdrawn just thirteen years later in May 1965. Behind *Clan Macgregor* is LMS Class 4 2-6-0 No 43045 which had been at Kingmoor since June 1963. Later moves saw it based at 10A Carnforth and 12D Workington. (D.K.Jones)

109) A man-made landscape dominates this picture taken at Great Rocks Quarry Junction, situated between Peak Forest Junction and Peak Forest station on 7th September 1957. Heading away from the camera light engine is former Midland Railway Class 3F 0-6-0 No 43290 (17D Rowsley) whilst on an opposite track LMS Fowler Class 4 2-6-4T No 42370, from 9D Buxton, powers a three-coach local passenger train. Both Nos 42370 and 43290 were but a memory by June 1962. (R.W.Hinton)

110) 8A Edge Hill (Liverpool) based LMS Class 5 4-6-0 No 45156 *Ayrshire Yeomanry* is a strange choice of engine to be employed as a station pilot at Birmingham (New Street), seen in platform 7 on 15th November 1964 during rebuilding work. Originally shedded in Scotland, No 45156 had been in England since April 1957. Although only four of these locomotives were ever named, *Ayrshire Yeomanry* was destined to survive until the end of steam. (J.Schatz)

111) When the LMS 'Compound' Class 4P 4-4-0's came to Scotland in the mid-1920's they were a significant advance in power over the native CR 4-4-0's. However, by 1934 the increasing weight of passenger trains outclassed the power of the 'Compounds', the real solution being the LMS Class 5 4-6-0's, one of which is outside 63A Perth shed on 7th August 1953. No 40923 had been laid aside, as indicated by the lack of a front end vacuum brake connection. (Peter Hay)

112) Just six months away from withdrawal and oblivion at the hands of Wards, Beighton, Sheffield, LMS *Jubilee* Class 4-6-0 No 45672 *Anson*, from 1A Willesden, is at rest in the shed yard at 1H Northampton on 10th May 1964 three months before being transferred to its final home at 5A Crewe (North). During its lengthy career, *Anson* also worked from the sheds at 3B Bushbury, 12B Carlisle (Upperby), 12A Carlisle (Kingmoor) and 2A Rugby. (Terry Ward)

113) First introduced in 1889, the Aspinall designed Lancashire & Yorkshire Class 2P 2-4-2 Tanks still numbered in excess of 100 units when taken into British Railway stock in January 1948. Some examples had enlarged bunkers which held four tons of coal instead of two. One of the latter engines, No 50887, from the nearby shed (26C), is on shunting duties at Bolton (Trinity Street) in August 1953, in the capable hands of a smiling crew member. (Peter Hay)

114) With a 'powder-puff' sky overhead a blustery wind catches the white exhaust fumes from the double chimney of LMS Class 4 2-6-0 No 43034, of 23C Lancaster, as it romps along at Hellifield with a local passenger duty on 24th March 1951. The double chimney as fitted to earlier examples of the class affected their steaming capacity and after tests which increased the steam production of the engines the double chimneys were discarded. (B.K.B.Green)

115) The eight-road former Caledonian Railway shed at Dawsholm was a ten-minute walk in grim surroundings from Maryhill (Central) station and was coded 65D from 1949 up until complete closure on 5th October 1964. Parked out of steam in front of the shed on 15th June 1958 is 65G Yoker based McIntosh Caledonian '29' Class (3F) 0-6-2T No 56238 which was built in 1895. Lurking inside the shed is locally allocated LMS Class 3 2-6-2T No 40158. (F.Hornby)

116) A lower quadrant signal bows its head and clears a path for LMS Class 3 2-6-2T No 40124 (9F Heaton Mersey) as it gingerly negotiates pointwork whilst crossing from one set of tracks to another with a five-coach local passenger train at Cheadle Heath in the fifties. These locomotives were to fall early victims to the introduction of diesel multiple units and were decimated by withdrawals in 1959. No 40124 was condemned in September 1961. (B.K.B.Green)

117) Work-stained and unkempt-looking, 2B Oxley based LMS Class 5 4-6-0 No 44812 bursts out of Wednesbury tunnel in the West Midlands and its exhaust echoes around the cutting as it blasts away at the head of a mineral train on 2nd August 1966. Upon the closure of Oxley shed in March 1967, No 44812 moved to a last abode at 5B Crewe (South), from whence it was withdrawn in September of the same year. It was scrapped at Cohens, Kettering. (T.R.Amos)

118) Steam locomotives, including a Beyer-Garratt 2-6-6-2T, are lined up as far as the eye can see at Crewe Works on 10th June 1951. The warm rays of the early summer sunshine reflect off the gleaming paintwork of two ex.works LMS Class 4 2-6-4 Tanks, one of which can be identified as No 42253, from 33A Plaistow in East London on the Eastern Region. By January 1957, No 42253 was at 34E Neasden, moving later on in life to 2F Woodford Halse on the GC. (B.K.B.Green)

119) Comparing the boiler sizes of these two ex. CR 0-6-0's we can see how power was increased as train loads grew in the 20th century. In fact the CR had some 0-8-0's, but they did not last as long as the 0-6-0 type because their length barred them from many a works or colliery siding. Class 3F No 57679 represents a late CR development of the 0-6-0's (1919) and is seen at 63B Stirling facing a 'Jumbo' of the previous century on 28th March 1959. (Peter Hay)

120) The driver of the prototype BR *Britannia* Class 4-6-2 No 70000 *Britannia*, from 5A Crewe (North), looks out of the cab as his charge puts in maximum effort as it climbs Shap unaided with a Warrington to Carlisle express in May 1965. Upon the closure of Crewe (North) to steam the following month, *Britannia* moved the short distance to the South shed (5B). Happily *Britannia* is still with us to this day preserved in full working order. (N.E.Preedy)

121) *Palestine* is constantly in the news nowadays and in 1961 its namesake, LMS *Jubilee* Class 4-6-0 No 45623, of 5B Crewe (South), is halted by a colour light signal whilst in charge of an empty stock working at Wigan (North Western) station. Once of 10B Preston, 8A Edge Hill (Liverpool), 5A Crewe (North) and 9A Longsight (Manchester), *Palestine* was reallocated to 26A Newton Heath in February 1962 and was condemned from there in August 1964. (D.K.Jones)

122) Based at 1A Willesden from December 1964 to September 1965, BR Class 4 2-6-0 No 76041 is seen at the shed in dreadful external condition on a sunny 15th June 1965. Two of the previous depots at which No 76041 was allocated were at 34E/14D Neasden and 14A Cricklewood. After leaving 1A it went to 2B Oxley, moving then to a final home at 6A Chester in early 1967 being withdrawn in April of the same year. It was scrapped at Cohens, Kettering in 1968. (D.K.Jones)

123) Although not taken out of traffic until much later in the year it is doubtful if Pickersgill Caledonian Class 3P 4-4-0 No 54506 ever turned a wheel in revenue earning service again. In this photograph, taken at its home shed 66D Greenock (Ladyburn) on 5th March 1961, it is paired with a large snowplough which is resting on some blocks of timber. After withdrawal in November 1961 No 54506 was stored at 66D until being despatched for scrapping in May 1963. (N.E.Preedy)

124) Newly transferred from 9J Agecroft, LMS Class 6P5F 2-6-0 No 42905 stands outside its new home at 9M Bury on 20th May 1964. This former Lancashire & Yorkshire depot only ever had a modest allocation at any one time and this consisted of a mixed variety of classes including a number of WD Class 8F 2-8-0's. The stay for No 42905 at Bury was shortlived, moving to 9G Gorton in October 1964. A final move in June 1965 took it to 9D Newton Heath. (D.K.Jones)

125) A senior member of the station staff at Forfar strides purposely forward as a Glasgow (Buchanan Street)-Aberdeen line express arrives on a dull 30th March 1964. In charge of the express, with steam to spare, is LNER A4 Class 4-6-2 No 60010 *Dominion of Canada*, from 61B Ferryhill (Aberdeen). Withdrawn from 61B in May 1965, No 60010 was later restored at Crewe Works before being shipped to Montreal, Canada for preservation. (D.K.Jones)

126) Two spotters note the number of LMS Class 2 2-6-2T No 41260, allocated locally at 24F, as it passes them under clear signals at the head of a local train at Fleetwood on 24th March 1957. In June 1961 this locomotive took its leave of the LMR, transferring to the Southern Region at 75A Brighton. It remained at 75A until June 1964, moving to 70F Bournemouth where it was withdrawn three months later and then cut up at P.Wood's yard in Queenborough, Kent. (B.K.B.Green)

127) Lengthy shadows creep across the station at Bletchley on 26th September 1953, where all of the signals in this picture are set at danger. Occupying one of the platforms is Fairburn designed LMS Class 4 2-6-4T No 42062 which was destined to spend many years based at 2A Rugby. In September 1964 it was drafted to 2K Bushbury and in April 1965 it went to a final home at 2J Aston. After a brief period at Aston it was rendered redundant. (B.K.B.Green)

128) One of the last depots to house the LMS Class 4F 0-6-0's in any numbers was at Workington, which was coded 12D (twice), 12C, 11B and 12F under BR. In light steam in front of the multi-road running shed on 11th June 1965 is No 44536. On this date there were no fewer than fifteen of these engines on Workington's books, these being Nos. 43953, 43964, 44061, 44157, 44160, 44310, 44346, 44356, 44449, 44451, 44462, 44489, 44505, 44536 and 44597. (Author's Collection)

129) An ex. North British Railway intruder, J35 Class 0-6-0 No 64520, is stabled in steam alongside the former Caledonian Railway four-road shed at 63C Forfar on 22nd June 1953. Forfar lost its parent status and code in November 1958 and became a sub-shed of 63A Perth, closing completely in July 1964. For No 64520 the future was bleak with condemnation looming in September 1959, from 65C Parkhead. It was scrapped at Kilmarnock Works. (B.K.B.Green)

130) There are more than ample supplies of coal in a bunker at the foot of the stairs for the signalmen within the wooden built signalbox at Cheadle Junction which is in dire need of a lick of fresh paint on a bright 26th July 1952. Passing the signalbox is LMS Class 2P 4-4-0 No 40683 at the head of a short local passenger working. In later years No 40683 was to be found at 2E Northampton, 24K Preston and 1C Watford prior to withdrawal in March 1961. (B.K.B.Green)

131) The spring sunshine welcomes the sight of 21A Saltley based LMS Class 5 4-6-0 No 44966 which looks in fine fettle as it accelerates away from Tamworth (High Level) and heads towards Burton-on-Trent and Derby with an express from Birmingham (New Street) on 19th April 1963. Allocated to Saltley from 22A Bristol Barrow Road in April 1957, No 44966 remained a firm favourite at the shed until April 1964 when it moved the short distance to 2J Aston. (T.R.Amos)

132) With an unidentified LMS Unrebuilt *Royal Scot* Class 4-6-0 in the left of the picture, LMS Class 4 2-6-4T No 42432 stands near to the paint shop at Crewe Works on 27th March 1949 after an overhaul. No 42432 will soon be steamed and returned to its home shed at 11A Carnforth. Records show us that this engine was still at Carnforth depot at the end of 1959, but then departed to a final abode at 12E/12C Barrow where it died in August 1965. (B.K.B.Green)

133) Home-based LMS Class 4P Compound 4-4-0 No 41152 poses in bright sunshine in the depot yard at Lancaster (Green Ayre) in the company of an 0-6-0 type on 24th March 1957. Hiding behind the smokebox door of No 41152 is War Department Class 8F 2-8-0 No 90205 which is a visitor to the shed from 26D Bury. Lancaster depot was unique on British Railways by having five different shedcodes from 1948-1966, these being 20H, 23C, 11E, 24J and 10J. (B.K.B.Green)

134) Four track workers are busy with their work as LMS Class 8F 2-8-0 No 48663, from 41E Staveley (Barrow Hill), passes the remote signalbox at Chinley East Junction and blackens the sky with exhaust fumes as it heads a loose-coupled freight train consisting of empty mineral wagons on 4th April 1960. No 48663 remained at Barrow Hill shed until November 1962, being drafted to a new and final home at 26F/9H Patricroft in Manchester. (N.E.Preedy)

135) Specially spruced-up for the occasion, former Caledonian Railway Class Drummond 2F 0-6-0 No 57441 (63A Perth) makes ready to depart from Alyth station (closed to passengers in 1951) for the return trip down the branch line to Alyth Junction with a joint RCTS/SLS special on a wet 16th June 1960. Although No 57441 (built in 1896) was not officially withdrawn until November 1961 it was stored at Forfar shed from February 1961 until October 1962. (F.Hornby)

136) Powering a lengthy excursion, LMS *Royal Scot* Class 4-6-0 No 46120 *Royal Inniskilling Fusilier*, of 5A Crewe (North), heads towards the camera at Hazel Grove on a dull 31st May 1954. In June 1958, No 46120 moved to 1B Camden, but was back at 5A three months later. Between June 1960 and June 1963 it served from the sheds at 9A Longsight (Manchester), 1B Camden, 1A Willesden and 6G Llandudno Junction. Its last days were spent at Crewe (North) again. (T.Lewis)

137) Scaffolding covers the large water tower like a spider's web in the righthand background of this picture taken at 26A Newton Heath on an overcast day in 1961. In steam in the foreground is a resident of 26A in the shape of LMS Class 8F 2-8-0 No 48716 which is paired with a smaller capacity Fowler tender. In January 1963, No 48716 was on the move to 26F Patricroft. Between then and withdrawal in August 1965 it had a further three transfers. (D.K.Jones)

138) The much rebuilt former Midland Railway Class 2P 4-4-0's originated with a Johnson design in 1882 yet formed the basis for a further 138 engines constructed during the years of the LMS. Hemmed between two other 'Midland' types on a sunny 19th August 1951 at 17A Derby is No 40444, of 20A Leeds (Holbeck). Although in ex.works condition, No 40444 had less than two years of active service to look forward to before being condemned in July 1953. (B.K.B.Green)

139) Captured in a bright shaft of sunlight, sulphur fumes lazily drift out of the funnel of LMS Class 8F 2-8-0 No 48519, which is a visitor to 9H Patricroft from 10A Carnforth on 11th July 1967. By this stage in time it was not uncommon for steam locomotives to be devoid of shedplates, as is the case with No 48519. A once longstanding inmate at 9D Buxton, No 48519 had been at Carnforth shed since September 1963. Its final abode was at 10F Rose Grove. (M.S.Stokes)

140) Looking south towards Etterby Junction we espy a filthy BR *Britannia* Class 4-6-2 No 70007 *Coeur-de-Lion* in steam in the yard at 12A Carlisle (Kingmoor) in July 1964. Inscribed on the smokebox door are the chalked words *'steam for ever'*. No 70007 had been at Kingmoor shed since moving from 31B March in December 1963. Prior to that it had been based at 32A Norwich for many years. Withdrawn in July 1965, No 70007 was scrapped at Crewe Works. (I.J.Hodson)

141) More Pacific power on show, this time of the LMS variety. Built at Crewe Works by BR in 1948, *Coronation* Class 4-6-2 No 46257 *City of Salford* was the final member of the class. Based at 12A Carlisle (Kingmoor), *City of Salford* pauses briefly at Crewe station in the summer of 1964 with a Chester to Euston express. Once of 1B Camden, this fine locomotive was allocated to 12B Carlisle (Upperby) from October 1958 until March 1961. (Kit Windle)

142) With an unidentified LMS Class 8F 2-8-0 for company, BR Class 5 4-6-0 No 73157 stands in the yard of its home shed at 1G Woodford Halse on 10th May 1964. From January 1957 until arriving at Woodford Halse in October 1963, No 73157 had worked from a variety of sheds - 34E/14D Neasden (three times), 34A Kings Cross, 41A Darnall (Sheffield), 17A Derby, 14A Cricklewood and 6A Chester. It worked from two more sheds prior to withdrawal in May 1968. (N.E.Preedy)

143) Possibly brand new, BR Class 4 2-6-4T No 80020 looks a fine sight in the yard at its home base of 66A Polmadie (Glasgow) on a bright 5th November 1951. Later allocated to the sheds at 61A Kittybrewster (Aberdeen), 67D Ardrossan and 67A Corkerhill (Glasgow), No 80020 only had a working life of some fourteen years before being condemned from the latter in June 1965. It was scrapped at the Motherwell Machinery & Scrap Co., Wishaw later in 1965. (N.E.Preedy)

144) The former London & North Western Railway Class 7F 0-8-0's were 1936 rebuilds of an earlier design in 1912 and by January 1957 the 200 or so survivors were allocated to a host of depots on the London Midland Region and from a handful of others on the Western Region. In early 1962, No 48930, from 21B Bescot, is captured on camera shunting at Walsall goods yard. Despite its fine external condition, No 48930 was withdrawn later in 1962.   (R.S.Carpenter)

145) 1A Willesden allocated LMS Class 5 4-6-0 No 45276 passes a row of grim looking terraced houses as it departs from Rugby (Midland) station with a fitted freight on a grey 27th March 1962. Once of 8A Edge Hill (Liverpool), 8B Warrington, 6J Holyhead and 6B Mold Junction, No 45276 had been at Willesden shed since June 1961. A final transfer took it to 5D Stoke in August 1963 where it remained until rendered redundant in January 1967. (D.K.Jones)

146) LMS *Jubilee* Class 4-6-0 No 45597 *Barbados*, of 55A Leeds (Holbeck), is photographed at speed between Bedford and Ampthill on the former Midland Railway main line with a rugby special from Leeds to London (St.Pancras) on 11th May 1963. Named after one of the islands in the West Indies, *Barbados* had been allocated to Holbeck shed for many years. It was to remain there until withdrawn in January 1965 after which it was scrapped at Drapers, Hull. (D.K.Jones)

147) Looking fresh from overhaul the paintwork on locally based ex. Caledonian Railway Pickersgill Class 3P 4-4-0 No 54505 gleams in the bright sunshine as it stands in the shed yard at 64D Carstairs on 16th May 1959. Access to this four-road open-ended depot was via a footbridge from Carstairs station. The lengthy, but narrow yard contained a turntable and a large concrete coaling plant. No 54505 was withdrawn from the shed in April 1961. (J.M.Tolson)

148) Bright sunshine envelopes former Midland Railway Class 2P 4-4-0 No 40337 and Beyer-Garratt Class 2-6-6-2T No 47971 in the yard of their home shed at 18C Hasland on 8th July 1951. For those brave enough to walk to this shed it would take almost an hour from Chesterfield (Midland) station. For years the single roundhouse was only partially covered giving little protection to the shed staff and locomotives during inclement weather. (B.K.B.Green)

149) LMS *Royal Scot* Class 4-6-0 No 46101 *Royal Scots Grey* (named after the oldest regiment in the British Army) speeds past Handforth Sidings, situated between Stockport and Wilmslow, with a Manchester (London Road) to Birmingham (New Street) express on 5th October 1952. No 46101 spent most of its career allocated to sheds associated with the West Coast Main Line. One exception was at 16D Annesley where it was based from January to September 1963. (R.W.Hinton)

150) With an unidentified LMS Class 3F 'Jinty' 0-6-0T in the right of the picture, LMS Ivatt Class 2 2-6-0 No 46454, from the nearby shed at 17A, is on station pilot duties at Derby on 8th September 1956. No 46454 departed from 17A in June 1957, moving the short distance to 17B Burton. After a spell at 15C Leicester (Midland) from July 1958 to September 1960, No 46454 returned to Derby again. A final move in November 1961 took it to 2E Saltley. (S.Dartnell)

151) Sunlight and shadow at 64C Dalry Road in 1957 where visiting LMS *Jubilee* Class 4-6-0 No 45617 *Mauritius*, from 5A Crewe (North), is being stocked-up with fresh coal supplies from the wooden coaler. *Mauritius* is devoid of its shedplate as it simmers patiently. Between October 1957 and condemnation in November 1964, No 45617 served from a number of different sheds on the LMR and was cut up at Wards, Beighton, Sheffield in April 1965. (D.K.Jones)

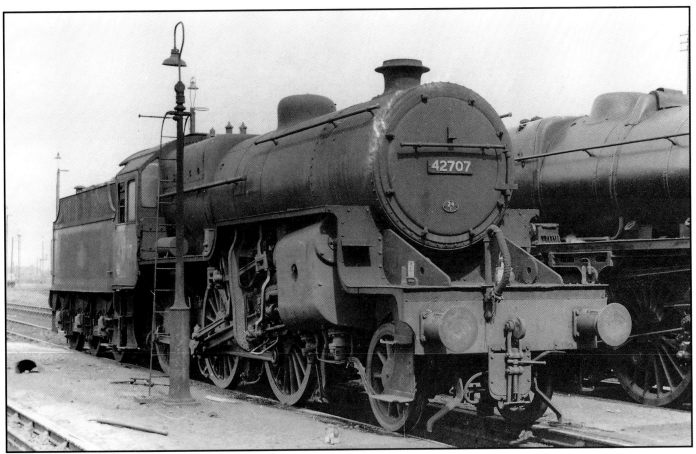

152) After a long period of time at 26A Newton Heath, LMS Class 6P5F 'Crab' 2-6-0 No 42707 found itself on the books at 24F Fleetwood by January 1960. In this photograph, taken on 12th August 1962, No 42707 is in the company of an LMS 'Black Five' 4-6-0 in front of the running shed at 24F. The following month it was despatched to Birmingham finding a new home at 21A Saltley where it remained until June 1964, moving to 8H Birkenhead. (J.Schatz)

153) The 'Old Order' at Crewe station long before the clutter associated with overhead electrified wires arrived. At the north end of the station an inmate of 5D Stoke, LMS Class 4 2-6-4T No 42233, is performing on a passenger duty on 10th September 1950 following an overhaul at Crewe Works. Over the years No 42233 was allocated to many sheds on the LMR, but in November 1966 it was drafted to the North Eastern Region, initially being based at 56A Wakefield. (B.K.B.Green)

154) The stonework and glass panels at Glasgow (Central) are stained with exhaust fumes from countless steam engines in 1961 as 66A Polmadie (Glasgow) allocated BR Class 4 2-6-4T No 80058, acting as a station pilot, departs with an empty coaching stock working. Polmadie shed had quite a number of these engines, used mostly on suburban workings. No 80058 was a Scottish based engine for all of its working life, being withdrawn from 66A in July 1966. (N.E.Preedy)

155) In spartan surroundings, LMS Class 5 4-6-0 No 44736, from 26A Newton Heath and in immaculate external condition, speeds towards the camera with an express duty at Cheadle Hulme on 27th February 1955. This locomotive remained at Newton Heath shed until January 1964 after which it was transferred to 9H Patricroft. Six months later it was on the move again, this time to 9K Bolton. Withdrawal for No 44736 came in September 1967. (B.K.B.Green)

156) Another immaculate looking LMS Class 5 4-6-0 No 44920 stands near to the concrete coaling plant after being refuelled at its home depot at 21A Saltley on a sunny 15th July 1951. No 44920 stayed at Saltley shed, with its multiple roundhouses, until May 1963, moving to 15C Leicester (Midland). Later transfers took No 44920 to 16C Derby, 16B Colwick, 8B Warrington and 8F Springs Branch Wigan. It was condemned from the latter in November 1967. (B.K.B.Green)

157) Another London Midland Region motive power depot with multiple roundhouses was at Nottingham, coded 16A and 16D under BR. On 26th June 1960 a number of engines are parked in bright sunshine in front of one the roundhouses, including resident former Midland Railway Class 2P 4-4-0 No 40421 which survived at this shed until withdrawal in January 1961, being scrapped at Looms, Spondon. Nottingham closed its doors to steam around April 1965. (N.E.Preedy)

158) Steam engines were employed as shunters at Crewe Works until October 1966 and amongst the types represented were LMS Class 2F, 3F and 4F 0-6-0's, LMS Class 3F 'Jinty' 0-6-0 Tanks, L & Y Class 3F 0-6-0's, L & Y Class 2F 0-6-0 Saddle Tanks, former Caledonian Railway Class 0F 0-4-0 Saddle Tanks and BR Class 2 2-6-2 Tanks. Off duty in the works yard on 17th June 1962 is L & Y 0-6-0 No 52093 which was withdrawn three months later and cut up at Crewe. (N.E.Preedy)

159) With a huge man-made slag-heap in the right of the frame, ex. Caledonian Railway Drummond Class 2F 0-6-0 No 57270, built in 1883, stands in front of the southern entrance to the open-ended eight-road shed at 66B Motherwell on 16th May 1959. This was one of the last Scottish sheds to house the Caledonian Class 2F and 3F 0-6-0's and on a visit by the author in November 1963 there were no less than thirteen examples to be seen, all in store. (J.M.Tolson)

160) The summer of 1967 was the last full one where enthusiasts could enjoy watching steam locomotives in action on passenger duties, particularly on the West Coast Main Line between Crewe and Carlisle. On 4th August 1967 the clouds are high in the sky as LMS Class 5 4-6-0 No 44911, from 12A Carlisle (Kingmoor), accelerates out of Preston with a Saturdays Only extra bound for Blackpool. Two months on in time and No 44911 was no longer with us. (N.E.Preedy)

161) An unkempt and bedraggled former Midland Railway Class 2F 0-6-0 No 58120, minus shedplate, leaks steam outside the shed at 8E Northwich in July 1960 not long after arriving from its former home at 8F Springs Branch Wigan. The authorities at Northwich were not impressed with No 58120 and it was returned to Springs Branch two months later. Despite its dreadful external condition, No 58120 was destined to continue in service until November 1962. (Ken Ellis)

162) Former London North Eastern Railway types were not uncommon visitors to Carlisle (Kingmoor) shed especially after the closure of Carlisle (Canal). On 17th June 1963, LNER inspired but BR built (1949) A1 Class 4-6-2 No 60160 *Auld Reekie*, from 64B Haymarket, basks in warm sunshine in the yard at the north end of 12A prior to taking up a working back to Edinburgh over the Waverley route. *Auld Reekie* was withdrawn at the end of 1963. (N.E.Preedy)

163) During the early fifties Derby was a good place to see former Midland Railway locomotives in abundance. With the depot and workshops in the background, Class 2P 4-4-0 No 40520, recently renumbered in LMS style, complete with the old logo on the tender, is seen in steam on 25th August 1952. Allocated to 55D Royston on the North Eastern Region, No 40520 was condemned from there in October 1957 and scrapped a month later at Derby. (Peter Hay)

164) With the fast flowing waters of the river Tay in the foreground, BR *Britannia* Class 4-6-2 No 70015 *Apollo*, of 9B Stockport, is unusually employed on a Glasgow to Dundee express as it departs from Perth with its safety valves lifting in September 1965. Once of 86C Cardiff (Canton), *Apollo* had moved to the LMR in July 1958 and served from a number of sheds including 9E Trafford Park, 26A Newton Heath and 6G Llandudno Junction. (Kit Windle)

165) The pride of 12B Carlisle (Upperby), LMS *Coronation* Class 4-6-2 No 46238 *City of Carlisle* is ready for the road in the yard at 66A Polmadie (Glasgow) sporting the headboard of *The Royal Scot* in August 1959. Constructed at Crewe Works in 1939, No 46238 was withdrawn in October 1964. Although Polmadie shed closed to steam on 1st May 1967 the author noted LMS Class 5 4-6-0 No 44862, from 12A Carlisle (Kingmoor), in steam there two months later (R.W.Hinton)

166) On a wet and gloomy day in the late fifties, LMS Unrebuilt *Patriot* Class 4-6-0 No 45520 *Llandudno* restarts a Manchester (London Road) to Birmingham (New Street) express from Stafford station. Based at 9A Longsight (Manchester), *Llandudno* was reallocated to 8A Edge Hill (Liverpool) in December 1960. Officially condemned in May 1962, No 45520 was stored at 24K Preston from November 1961 onwards before being scrapped at Crewe in June 1962. (R.S.Carpenter)

167) Having acknowledged the 'right away' from the guard, the driver of LMS Class 5 4-6-0 No 45437, shedded locally at 12A Kingmoor, releases high pressure steam as his steed departs from Carlisle (Citadel) station with a southbound relief express on 12th August 1967. Like many others of the class, No 45437 was based at a host of sheds over the preceeding years, including 6J Holyhead, 5D Stoke, 26A Newton Heath, 9J Agecroft and 10A Carnforth. (D.K.Jones)

168) In lined livery, LMS Fowler Class 3 2-6-2T No 40013 is in the yard of its home shed at 26A Newton Heath in the company of an unidentified L & Y Class 2F 0-6-0ST on 22nd August 1954. Withdrawn from Newton Heath shed in December 1959, No 40013 was stored at the west main line, Derby until February 1960 before being despatched to Doncaster Works for cutting up. Newton Heath shed ceased its long association with steam traction on 1st July 1968. (B.K.B.Green)

169) Brilliant sunshine highlights the exterior of LMS *Royal Scot* Class 4-6-0 No 46119 *Lancashire Fusilier* as it lifts its safety valves prior to departing from Stockport (Edgeley) station with an express in 1961. *Lancashire Fusilier*, allocated to 8A Edge Hill (Liverpool), had been at this depot since a move from 5A Crewe (North) in November 1958. It was to remain at 8A until rendered surplus to operating requirements in November 1963. (R.W.Hinton)

170) This is a fine panoramic view of the Derbyshire countryside in high summer. Rounding a curve at Milford, LMS *Jubilee* Class 4-6-0 No 45682 *Trafalgar*, from 22A Bristol Barrow Road, heads the down *Devonian* express on 5th August 1955. Apart from a brief foray at 19B Millhouses (October to November 1957) *Trafalgar* was destined to spend the remainder of its working life at Barrow Road shed, which became the property of the Western Region in 1958. (R.W.Hinton)

171) With the mark of impending doom, a sacked chimney, it looks as though it is the end of the road for former Midland Railway Class 2F 0-6-0 No 58215 which is dead on an isolated weed-strewn track at 15D Bedford in August 1957. However, all was not lost. In February 1958, No 58215 was resurrected from the dead and transferred to 12B Carlisle (Upperby). Two years later, in February 1960, it was on the move again, this time to 2A Rugby. (N.E.Preedy)

172) Equipped with a double chimney, Caprotti valve gear and Timken Roller bearings, 20A Leeds (Holbeck) allocated LMS Class 5 4-6-0 No 44755 looks an awesome sight in the yard at 17A Derby on 19th August 1951. Despite having youth on their side, the experimental Class 5 Caprotti engines tended to fall early victims to withdrawal. No 44755 (1948) was withdrawn from 9B Stockport in November 1963 and scrapped at Crewe Works in February 1964. (B.K.B.Green)

173) Glasgow (St.Enoch) station is enveloped in bright sunshine on 1st September 1952. In the foreground is former Caledonian Railway Class 3P 4-4-0 No 54479, from 66D Greenock (Ladyburn). In the background is LMS Class 2P 4-4-0 No 40651 which survived in service until November 1961. Although not condemned until October 1959, No 54479 was placed in store with some sister engines at Princess Pier, Greenock shortly after this picture was taken. (Peter Hay)

174) We take our leave of BRITISH RAILWAYS STEAMING ON THE LONDON MIDLAND REGION - Volume 5 with this fine photograph of LMS Class 5 4-6-0 No 44990, of 56F Low Moor, which is being deployed on shed pilot duties at 24E Blackpool Central on 24th March 1957. This large eight-road depot, situated near to Blackpool Football Club, hosted engines from many parts of BR during the summer months and the annual Illuminations until closed in September 1964. (B.K.B.Green)